SIMPLY STUNNING CROCHETED BAGS

DEAR READER

The great thing about crochet is that you can create so many different patterns and designs with just a few basic stitches. By using a bright selection of yarns, there's almost no limit to the colourful creations you can make.

In this book, we combine fabulous patterns and colours with trendy bag designs. From shopping bags and laundry bags to beach bags and elegant totes, there's so much to choose from! Discover patterns ranging from soft harmonious shades to the fantastically bright and eye-catching.

The instructions include useful illustrations and diagrams and a basic crochet course at the beginning of the book explains all the basic techniques you will need to know. The important thing is to keep being creative!

These projects are made up of some of our favourite designs – we hope you enjoy making them.

The Editors

CONTENTS

Levels of difficulty

● = easy

●● = requires a little practice

●●● = more challenging

BASIC CROCHET COURSE

Casting on

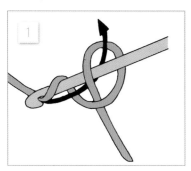

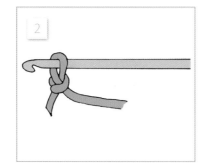

Chain (ch)

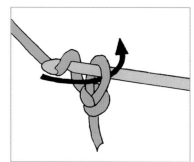

Every piece of crochet starts with a knot. The knot is not counted as a stitch when working a row of chain stitches. Start by threading the yarn in a loop.

Insert the hook through the loop, yarn over hook and draw through. Pull on the thread so the loop tightens. It should still be loose, but not so loose that it slips off the hook.

Hook through the loop and wind the yarn that is around your index finger from back to front around the hook (yarn over hook). Draw the yarn through the loop.

Magic ring

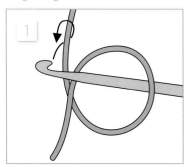

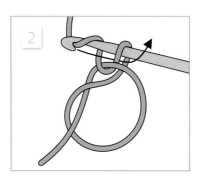

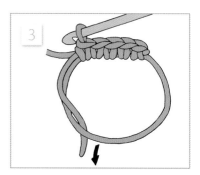

Yarn in a loop, insert hook, yarn over hook and draw through. Do not tighten the loop just yet. Wind the working yarn around your left index finger.

Hold the point where the loop crosses between thumb and middle finger, make a loop, and draw through the ring on the hook.

Work the stitches around the loop according to the instructions (our example uses sc/UK dc). Close the round with a slip stitch into the first stitch, then tighten the yarn loop at the beginning.

Slip stitch (slst)

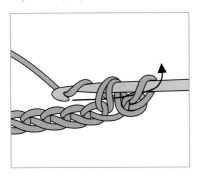

Insert hook into both loops on the stitch and draw yarn through. Unlike the sc (*UK dc*), draw this loop straight through the stitch and the loop that is on the hook.

Single crochet (sc)/ *UK double (UK dc)*

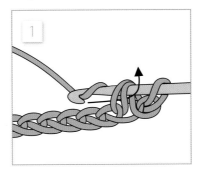

Insert hook in both parts of the stitch and draw yarn through (wind over hook from back to front). Draw this loop through the stitch loops.

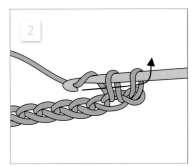

You should now have two loops on the hook. Draw yarn through again and through both of the loops on the hook. This last step finishes the stitch, and is also referred to as 'finishing a stitch' (for all types of stitch).

Half double crochet (hdc)/ *UK half treble (htr)*

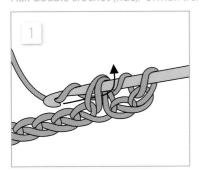

Yarn over hook (wrap yarn from back to front around the hook), then insert the hook in both stitch loops. Draw yarn through (yarn over hook) and draw through the stitch loops.

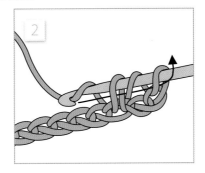

As with the double crochet (*UK tr*), you will now have three loops on the hook. Yarn over hook again, and draw through all three loops on the hook in one move (unlike a double crochet /*UK treble*, where you do this step in two moves) to finish the stitch.

Double crochet (dc)/ *UK treble (tr)*

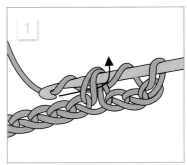

Replace the first dc (*UK tr*) in a row with 3 ch. Yarn over hook, and insert hook in the fourth stitch from the hook. Yarn over hook, and draw through the stitch.

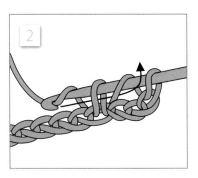

Draw yarn through again, and through two of the three loops on the hook.

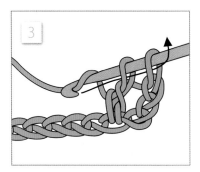

Draw yarn through again and through the two remaining loops on the hook finishing the stitch. Work all the following dc (*UK tr*) in the next stitches (unless the instructions say otherwise).

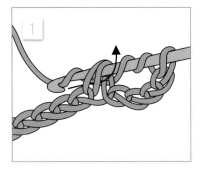

Replace the first treble (*UK dtr*) in the row with 4 ch. Yarn over hook twice, and insert in the fifth stitch from the hook. Yarn over hook. Draw this loop through.

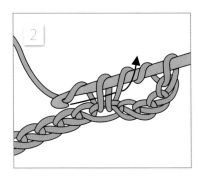

You should now have a total of four loops on the hook. Yarn over hook again. Draw this loop through two of the four loops.

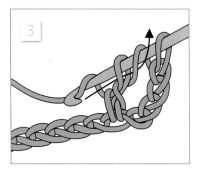

You will now have three loops on the hook. Yarn over hook again. Draw this loop through two of the three loops on the hook.

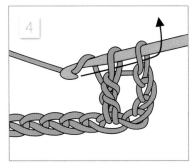

Yarn around hook once again. Draw this loop through the last two loops on the hook.

Double treble (dtr)/ *UK triple treble (trtr)* are worked in the same way, except that you start with three loops instead of two at the beginning.

Relief double crochet (rdc)/
UK relief treble (UK rtr) from front

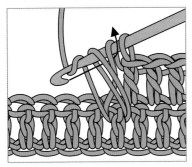

Yarn over hook, then push the hook around the front of the dc (*UK tr*) in the previous row. Draw yarn through and around the dc (*UK tr*). Draw yarn through twice more and through two loops, twice. (You can work other stitches in the same way.)

Decrease (dec) several
stitches together

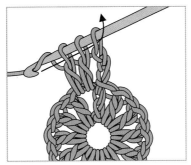

Work the number of stitches in the same or several stitches as far as the final step. You will work this final step at the same time for all of the stitches: yarn over hook, and draw through all the loops.

Work several stitches in
the same stitch

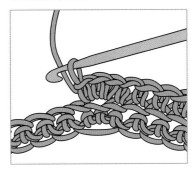

Work several stitches in succession, all of them into the same stitch of the previous row. The picture shows sc (*UK dc*), as an example.

Decrease 2 dc (*UK tr*)
in 1 stitch

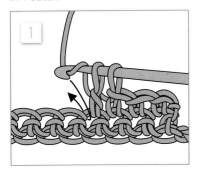

Work a dc (*UK tr*) until you have two loops left on the hook. Do not finish this stitch just yet, but …

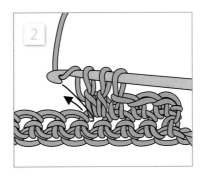

… crochet another dc (*UK tr*) into the same stitch without completing it. Now complete both of these stitches together.

Finishing your work

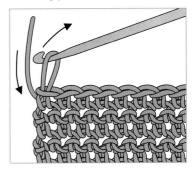

When you get to the very last stitch, cut the yarn to leave a length of approximately 6in (15cm), which you will then weave in. Pull this yarn through the last stitch and tighten. This is your finishing knot.

HANDBAG IN APRICOT

Size: approximately 11¾ x 9¾in (30 x 25cm) without straps • Level of difficulty ●

Materials:
- Cotton yarn (100% recycled cotton: 35¼oz /1000g) in apricot (note: because the material thickness varies, the finished size may vary slightly)
- 1 sew-on magnetic clasp, ¾in (2cm) diameter
- 1 brown leather handle with end hooks
- O/16 (12mm) crochet hook

Basic pattern 1
Rows of sc (*UK dc*), working only into the back loop of the stitch in the previous row. Start each row with 1 additional ch.

Basic pattern 2
Work in sc (*UK dc*), starting each row or round with 1 additional ch. Finish each round with 1 slst into the first sc (*UK dc*).

Gauge in basic pattern 1
7 sc (*UK dc*) x 8 rows = 4 x 4in (10 x 10cm)

HOW TO DO IT
For the **body of the bag**, work 30 ch + 1 turning ch, then work 20 rows in basic pattern 1. Fold this item in half and sew up the side seams. Crochet 2 rounds of 34 stitches around the top edge in basic pattern 2.

For the **flap**, work 3 rows of 17 stitches in basic pattern 2 over the first 17 stitches of the previous round. Then work 4 more rows in basic pattern 2, decreasing 2 stitches together on both sides of each row = 9 stitches. Work sc (*UK dc*) around the flap.

Finishing off: Sew on the magnetic catch and insert the handle.

PASTEL MESH BAG

Level of difficulty ● ●

Materials:

- Wool blend (70% new wool, 30% polyamide, length
  54½yd/3½oz, 50m/100g): approximately 9oz (250g)
  in orange-pink-green marl
- N/15 (10mm, UK 000) and
  O/16 (12mm) crochet hooks
- 11 (8mm, UK 0) knitting needles
- Sewing needle
- Sewing thread in a matching colour

Basic pattern

Work ch and sc (*UK dc*) in rounds. Start each round with 1
ch to replace the first sc (*UK dc*), and join to the starting ch
with 1 slst to close.

HOW TO DO IT

Start by making a magic ring (see page 4). Use your N/15
(10mm, UK 000) hook to draw the working thread
through the loop and work 1 ch. **Round 1:** Work 13 sc (*UK
dc*) into the ring. Close the round with 1 slst in the first sc
(*UK dc*), and tighten the loop. **Round 2:** Work 5 ch and 1
sc (*UK dc*) into each sc (*UK dc*) of the previous round.
Rounds 3-14: Work 5 ch and 1 sc (*UK dc*) around each
ch arch.

Knit the straps. Cast on 3 stitches and knit as follows. *Knit
3, then push the knitting back to the beginning so the
yarn is behind the knitting, then repeat from *until the
work measures 23½in (60cm). Work the second strap in
the same way.

Finishing off: Sew the straps to the top of the bag.

FLORAL BAG

Size: approximately 15¼ x 10¼in (39 x 26cm) without handles • Level of difficulty ● ● ●

Materials:

- Cotton blend (60% cotton, 40% polyacrylic, length 153yd/1¾oz, 140m/50g): 5½oz (150g) each in pink and orange, 1¾oz (50g) in green
- H/8 (5mm, UK 6) crochet hook
- 1 pair bag handles
- If required, sewing needle and matching thread

Basic pattern

Work a length of ch, and then work in rows of tr (*UK dtr*). Work the first tr (*UK dtr*) in row 1 into the fifth ch from the hook. Replace the first tr (*UK dtr*) in each row with 4 ch. Work 1 tr (*UK dtr*) into each tr (*UK dtr*).

Gauge in basic pattern

18 tr (*UK dtr*) x 7 rows = 4 x 4in (10 x 10cm)
1 crocheted square = 5 x 5in (13 x 13cm)

HOW TO DO IT

Work 6 crocheted squares 1a and 1b as follows: Crocheted square 1a: Crochet 8 ch in pink. Join together with 1 slst, and work as shown in pattern 2 (page 15). Replace the first stitch of each round with the number of ch shown in the pattern, or work one additional ch before a sc (*UK dc*) at the beginning of a round. After rounds 2/4 continue with the 2 or 4 larger ch stitches shown at the beginning of rounds 3/5. Watch out for the sc (*UK dc*) that are inserted lower in rounds 3, 5 and 7. Work the rsc (*UK rdc*) of round 5 from back to front around the lower sc (*UK dc*) of round 3, and the rsc (*UK rdc*) of round 7 from back to front around the rsc (*UK rdc*) of round 5. After round 6 cut the thread, and for round 7 (shown in light grey) join the green yarn at arrow a. Cut the thread at the end of round 7. For rounds 8–10 join the pink yarn at arrow b. Work rounds 1–20 once.

Crocheted square 1b: Work as **crocheted square 1a**, but in orange instead of pink. ▶

Finishing off: Arrange the crocheted squares as shown in the diagram in four rows of three squares, and sew together neatly using a blunt embroidery needle so the seams are completely flat. Then fold the large rectangle in half with the wrong sides together and sew up the side seams. Attach the handles to the middle of the top edge, as shown in the picture.

Tip: If you would like to make the bag stronger, line it in some matching fabric. Cut out a rectangle the size of the 3 x 4 crocheted squares, then fold in half with the wrong sides facing and sew up the side seams, either on a sewing machine or by hand. Put the fabric bag inside the crocheted bag and line up the side seams. Fold the top edge of the fabric bag over by about ½in (1cm), and sew along the folded edge by hand in sewing thread and using tiny stitches. Then work 2 rows of dc (*UK tr*) in orange or pink along the top edge.

Crochet Pattern 1

1a	1b	1a
1b	1a	1b
1a	1b	1a
1b	1a	1b

Symbols

1a = 1 crocheted square 1a
1b = 1 crocheted square 1b

Crochet pattern 2

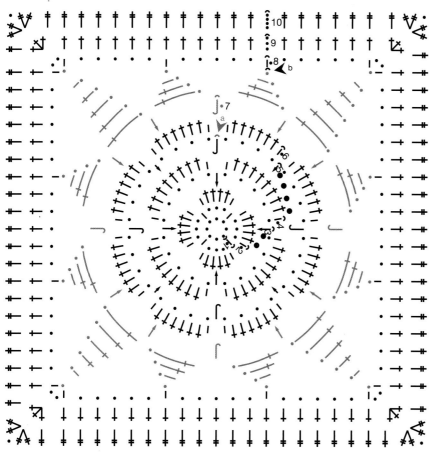

Symbols

• = 1 ch

⌢ = 1 slst

ı = 1 sc (*UK dc*)

ȷ = 1 sc (*UK dc*), worked from behind between the dc (*UK tr*) of the previous round and around the ch arch

⌡ = 1 rsc (*UK rdc*)

† = 1 dc (*UK tr*)

‡ = 1 tr (*UK dtr*)

If the symbols are joined at the bottom, this means the stitches are worked into the same stitch of the previous round.

If the stitches are joined at the top, it means that the corresponding stitches are decreased together.

BEACH BAG

Materials:
- Rayon raffia, matt (length 22yd (20m)/skein): approximately 10 strands each in yellow, orange and red
- 7 (4.5mm, UK 7) and I/9 (5.5mm, UK 5) crochet hooks
- Darning or sewing needle

Basic pattern

Work sc (*UK dc*) in continuous rounds without a beginning or end. Mark the round transitions with a piece of thread. To double 1 stitch, work 2 sc (*UK dc*) into the same stitch. When changing colours, finish the last stitch in one colour in the new colour.

Colour sequence

9 strands in yellow, 9 strands in orange and 8 strands in red.

HOW TO DO IT

For the main part of the bag, work 26 ch + 1 turning ch with a 7 (4.5mm, UK7) hook in the yellow raffia. Round 1: Work sc (*UK dc*) along both sides of the length of ch, working 3 stitches (corners) into the first and last stitches. Continue in sc (*UK dc*), increasing at the corners as follows: Round 2: Double the 3 corner stitches. Round 3: Double the 6 corner stitches = 12 stitches. Round 4: Double 1 stitch either side of the 4 middle corner stitches. Rounds 5–7: Continue without increasing. Round 8: Continue with a I/9 (5.5mm, UK 5) hook. From round 9: For further increases, double the stitches either side of the middle 4 corner stitches, working once in rounds 10 and 11, then 8 in every third round, 1 in the fourth round, 3 in every fifth round. Finish after 17¼in (44cm) or when you have finished the raffia.

For the straps (make 2), work 25 ch in yellow, 18 ch in orange, 100 ch in red, 18 ch in orange, and 25 ch in yellow, and continue working sc (*UK dc*) in these colours until the strap is of the desired width.

The straps go all the way down to the bottom, which makes the bag more stable. Sew the straps onto the inside with the matching colours lined up, starting and finishing at the bottom of the bag.

SUMMER BAG

Level of difficulty ● ● ●

Materials:

- Cotton yarn (100% cotton, length 137yd/1¾oz, 125m/50g): 1¾oz (50g) each in bright green, turquoise, green, dark green, olive green, aqua, white and brown
- D/3 (3mm, UK 11) and E/4 (3.5mm/UK 9) crochet hooks
- 48 crochet rings, flat, 1⅜in (36mm) diameter
- 1 pair bag handles

Colour sequence

*Brown, turquoise, green, olive green, bright green, white, aqua, dark green, repeating from *.

HOW TO DO IT

Work 40 sc (*UK dc*) around the **crochet rings** with the D/3 (3mm, UK 11) crochet hook, either to the colour sequence in the photo or your own choice. Cut the yarn, leaving long threads with which to sew the rings together. Along the bottom edge of the two **bag handles,** use the E/4 (3.5mm, UK 9) crochet hook to work sc (*UK dc*) in stripes. Work 42 ch and then the rows in the colour sequence given above. After 13 rows, place the work around the handle and crochet the two sides together. Crochet along the side edges in the same colour.

Sew a row of 6 crochet rings onto the handles, then a row of 8 crochet rings, and below that 1 row of 10 crochet rings. Refer to the illustration for the colour sequence or choose your own.

Crochet the **side pieces** directly to the lower row of rings. Work 5 sc (*UK dc*) on each ring, and leave 8 ch between each of the rings. Repeat until the last ring, then work 1 ch to turn. Work the return row in sc (*UK dc*), still working in the same colour sequence. Finish after 22 rows.

Work the other side in the same way.

For the **bottom of the bag**, work 2 ch and then work 2 sc (*UK dc*) in the next row. Continue working sc (*UK dc*) in the colour sequence, increasing 1 stitch at the beginning of each row until there are 22 stitches in a row. Work 96 rows without increasing. From row 97 miss 1 stitch at the beginning of each row until there are 2 stitches left in a row, then finish.

Finishing off: Sew the bottom of the bag to the sides, folding the bottom corners of the side pieces in to make a rounded shape.

BLUE CLUTCH BAG

Size: approximately 9½ x 4¾in (24 x 12cm) · Level of difficulty ● ●

Materials:

- Cotton blend (59% cotton, 41% viscose, length 115yd/1¾oz, 105m/50g): 3½oz (100g) in blue, scraps in light blue and white
- 2 pieces blue fleece, 9½ x 4 ¾in (24 x 12cm)
- Firm card (for the back), 8¾ x 4in (22 x 10cm)
- G/6 (4mm, UK 8) crochet hook
- Knitting dolly

Basic pattern

Work in rows as shown in pattern 1. Start each row with 3 ch to replace the first dc (*UK tr*) or with 1 additional ch before the first hdc (*UK htr*). Work the stitches before the pattern, then keep repeating the pattern and finish with the stitches after the pattern.

Gauge in basic pattern

19 stitches x 12 rows = 4 x 4in (10 x 10cm)

HOW TO DO IT

To make the **bag**, work 46 ch + 1 turning ch in blue, then work rows 1–5 of the basic pattern. Repeat rows 4 and 5 four more times (= front), then work rows 6 and 7 seven times (= base and back). Work rows 4 and 5 six times, and finish with row 4 (= flap) = 40 rows.

For the **side pieces** (make 2), 9 ch + 1 turning ch, and then work row 1 of the basic pattern. Then work rows 6 and 7 six times = 13 rows.

For the **strap**, use a knitting dolly to knit a 31½in (80cm) cord in blue following the manufacturer's instructions.

Fold the bag together with the wrong sides facing. Place the side pieces between the front and back and against the base with the wrong sides facing, and join together on the right sides in sc (*UK dc*). Work several stitches into the corner stitches so that the seam continues around the corners without pulling. Work sc (*UK dc*) around the side edges of the flap.

Finishing off: Work the flower to pattern 2 and sew on as shown in the photo. Sew the knitted cord to the tops of the side pieces. ▶

Flower

Work 5 ch in white and join in a ring with a slst. **Round 1:** 1 ch to replace the first sc (*UK dc*), then 7 sc (*UK dc*) in the ch ring. End the round with 1 slst into the first sc (*UK dc*). Work **round 2** in light blue as shown in pattern 2, starting with 1 slst. Finish after round 2.

Tip: To reinforce the **back**, place the pieces of fleece together with the right sides facing, then sew (either by hand or by machine) along three sides with a seam allowance of about ½in (1cm). Turn right side out and iron. Push the card into the sleeve. Fold the seam allowances to the inside and sew up the turning opening by hand. Place the reinforcement in the middle of the wrong side (= inside) in the back section, and stitch in place by hand using small stitches.

Crochet pattern 1

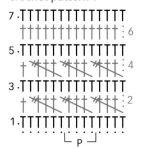

Crochet pattern 2

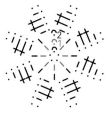

Symbols

·	= 1 ch	
⌒	= 1 slst	
I	= 1 sc (*UK dc*)	
T	= 1 hdc (*UK htr*)	
†	= 1 dc (*UK tr*)	
⋇††	= miss 1 stitch in previous row, 3 dc (*UK tr*), 1 tr (*UK dtr*) back into the missed stitch	
P	= pattern	

SHOULDER BAG

Size: approximately 19¾ x 9¾in (50 x 25cm) • Level of difficulty ● ●

Materials:
• Cotton blend (75% cotton, 25% viscose, length
  120yd/1¾oz, 110m/50g):12oz (350g) in grey, 3½oz
  (100g) in white and 5oz (150g) in natural
• 100in (250cm) cord in natural, ½in (1cm) diameter
• 3 magnetic catches, ¾in (2cm) diameter
• J/10 (6mm, UK 4) crochet hook

Basic pattern 1
Work in sc (*UK dc*) with double yarn, starting each row or
round with 1 additional ch. Finish each round with 1 slst
into the first sc (*UK dc*). To change colours, finish the last
stitch in the new colour. ▶

Basic pattern 2

Work hdc (*UK htr*) with double yarn, starting each row or round with 1 additional ch. Finish each round with 1 slst into the first hdc (*UK htr*). To change colours, finish the last stitch in the new colour.

Colour sequence

5 rounds in grey, 3 rounds in white, 1 round in grey, 5 rounds in natural, 2 rounds in grey, 1 round in natural, 1 round in grey, 1 round in white, 4 rounds in grey.

Gauge in basic pattern 1

15 stitches x 16 rows = 4 x 4in (10 x 10cm)

Gauge in basic pattern 2

14 stitches x 10 rows = 4 x 4in (10 x 10cm)

HOW TO DO IT

For the **base of the bag**, work 25 ch + 1 turning ch in grey, then work 54 rows in basic pattern 1. After row 54, work 158 hdc (*UK htr*) in grey around the bottom of the bag, and finish the round with 1 slst = **round 1. Round 2:** Work 1 rdc (*UK rtr*) from behind around each hdc (*UK htr*) of the previous round (= hdc (*UK htr*), inserting the hook from back to front around the stitch in the previous round). **Rounds 3–25:** Work in basic pattern 2 in the colour sequence, decreasing every ninth and tenth stitch together in the third round = 143 stitches. **Rounds 26–27:** Work sc (*UK dc*) in grey.

For the add-on pockets (make 2), 22 ch + 1 additional turning ch in grey, then work 13 rows in basic pattern 2 in the following colour sequence: 2 rows in grey, 3 rows in white, 1 row in grey, 5 rows in natural, 2 rows in grey.

For the loops (make 6), work 5 rows of 4 stitches in natural to basic pattern 1.

Finishing off: Sew the pockets and loops onto the bag as shown in the photo, then draw the cord through the loops and knot the ends. Fold the two sides of the bag to the inside by 2½in (6cm), and secure each with 1 magnetic catch. Sew the third magnetic catch out of sight under the middle loop.

BROWN BASKET BAG

Size: 15 x 16½in (38 x 42cm) • Level of difficulty ● ●

Materials:
- Cotton blend (53% cotton, 47% linen, length 93yd/1¾oz, 85m/50g): 8¾oz (250g) in brown
- D/3 (3mm, UK 11) crochet hook

Basic pattern
Work sc (*UK dc*) in rounds, with 1 ch at the beginning of each round to replace the first sc (*UK dc*), and join to the replacement ch with 1 slst. To double 1 stitch, work 2 sc (*UK dc*) into the same stitch.

Mesh
Round 1: *1 sc (*UK dc*), 3 ch, miss 2 stitches, repeat from * to the end of the round. Round 2: Do not close round 1, but work 3 ch and move to the next round, working the first sc (*UK dc*) into the first ch arch of round 1, then alternately work 3 ch and 1 sc (*UK dc*) into the next ch arch. Continue working in spirals in this fashion.

Gauge
18 sc (*UK dc*) x 20 rows = 4 x 4in (10 x 10cm)

HOW TO DO IT
For the base, work 3 ch and join with a slst. Then work in the basic pattern as follows:
Round 1: Work 4 sc (*UK dc*) into the ring. Round 2: Double every stitch = 8 stitches.
Round 3: Double every second stitch = 12 stitches. Round 4: Double every third stitch = 16 stitches. Round 5: Double every fourth stitch = 20 stitches. Continue in this way, increasing 4 sc (*UK dc*) in every round until you have about 7 ½in (19cm) measured from the middle.
For the sides in the mesh, crochet 7in (18cm), then return to the basic pattern for the top trim. For the top trim, work 3 sc (*UK dc*) around each ch arch in the first round. When you have worked 2in (5cm), start the strap. Continue working in rows across 4in (10cm) on the edge, starting each row with 1 additional turning ch and omitting the last stitch in each row until the strap is only about 2¼in (5.5cm) wide. Continue working without decreasing until the strap measures 21¾in (55cm). Now work the second half of the strap on the opposite side in exactly the same way. Sew the ends of the strap together.

SHOULDER BAG IN KHAKI

Size: approximately 13½ x 10¼in (34 x 26cm) • Level of difficulty ● ●

Materials:
- Polyester yarn (100% polyamide, length approximately 63yd/1¾oz, 58m/50g): 12oz (350g) in khaki
- G/6 (4mm, UK 8) crochet hook
- Sewing needle
- Sewing thread in a matching colour

Basic pattern 1
Work sc (*UK dc*) in rows, with 1 ch at the beginning of each row to replace the first sc (*UK dc*).

Basic pattern 2
Work dc (*UK tr*) in rows, starting each row with 3 ch to replace the first dc (*UK tr*).

HOW TO DO IT

For the front inside, work 54 ch + 1 turning ch, then work 10¼in (26cm) in basic pattern 2: dc (*UK tr*). Then for the base, work 2in (5cm) in basic pattern 1: sc (*UK dc*), and for the back 10¼in (26cm) in basic pattern 2. Work ½in (1cm) along the top edge in basic pattern 1. Then for the flap, work 9½in (24cm) in the lacy pattern as shown in the diagram. The pattern repeat consists of 9 stitches. Turn the rows as described above. Keep repeating the pattern and rows 2 to 7.

For the sides and the strap (make 1), work 8 ch + 1 turning ch. Work 64in (162cm) in basic pattern 1. Sew the narrow sides of the strap to the base, to both sides of the front inside and to the back. Steam the seams.

Tip: If you prefer, sew a zip in the top edge of the front and back for added security; it will be concealed by the flap.

Crochet pattern

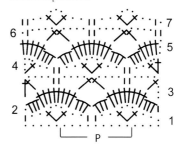

Symbols

- · = 1 ch
- I = 1 sc (*UK dc*)
- T = 1 hdc (*UK htr*)
- † = 1 dc (*UK tr*)
- ᐯ = 2 dc (*UK tr*) in same stitch
- ⋏ = dec 2 dc (*UK tr*) tog
- ⋎ = 1 dc (*UK tr*), 3 ch, 1 dc (*UK tr*) in same stitch
- P = pattern

OLIVE SHOULDER BAG

Size: 12½ x 8in (32 x 20.5cm) (bag) • Level of difficulty ● ● ●

Materials:

- Polyester yarn (100% polyamide, length approximately 109yd/1¾oz, 100m/50g): 5oz (150g) in olive marl
- G/6 (4mm, UK 8) crochet hook
- 1 long button made of a natural material (make sure the holes are big enough)
- Sewing needle
- Black sewing thread
- Lining or cotton, approximately 31½ x 19¾in (80 x 50cm), in black (optional)

Basic pattern 1

Work in rows in accordance with the pattern, starting each row with 1 ch to replace the first sc (*UK dc*).

Basic pattern 2

Work dc (*UK tr*) in rows, starting each row with 3 ch to replace the first dc (*UK tr*).

Gauge

24.5 dc (*UK tr*) x 15 rows = 4 x 4in (10 x 10cm)

HOW TO DO IT

Work the **front and back** across, starting with 52 ch, 1 turning ch and 3 ch for the first base. Work the stitches shown in the diagram once. Work rows 1–15 upwards once, then repeat rows 8–15 twice, and finish with rows 8–24. Finish after 48 rows (= approximately 12½in (32cm). For the **shoulder strap** (work 1), start with 10 ch + 3 turning ch. Work in basic pattern 2. Finish after 60in (150cm) or when you have reached the desired length. Sew up the narrow ends of the strap. Place the strap on the middle and sew between the front and back (as the base and side), starting in the middle of the base. ▶

Finishing off: Line the bag with black fabric if desired. To close the bag, make a tassel out of 10 threads approximately 9¾in (25cm) long. Crochet a length of chain to it.

Sew the long button to the length of chain, and attach the end to the middle of the top on the back of the bag. Crochet a chain arch on the front.

Crochet pattern

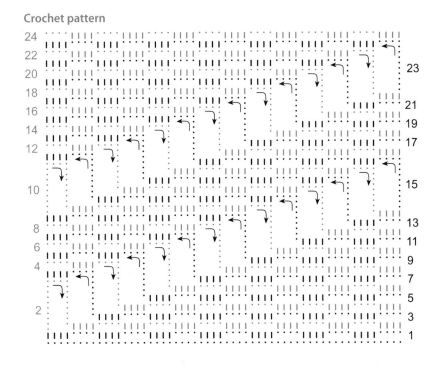

Symbols

- · = 1 ch
- I = 1 sc (UK dc)
- → = direction of crochet

GRANNY SQUARE BAG

Size: approximately 14¼ x 16¼in (36 x 41cm) without strap · Level of difficulty ● ●

Materials:
- Pure new wool (100% Merino wool, length 164yd/1¾oz, 150m/50g): approximately 1¾oz (50g) each in fuchsia, mallow, pale yellow, pale pink and gold
- 1 black fabric bag
- G/6 (4mm, UK 8) crochet hook
- Sewing needle
- Black sewing thread

Basic pattern in rows
Work to pattern 1 (see page 34). Start each row with 3 ch to replace the first dc (UK tr). Work the stitches before the pattern, then keep repeating the pattern and finish with the stitches after the pattern.

Basic pattern in rounds
Work to pattern 2 (see page 34). Start each round with 3 ch to replace the first dc (UK tr), and end with 1 slst into the third replacement ch. Work the stitches before the pattern, then keep repeating the pattern and finish with the stitches after the pattern.

Square
Work 6 ch and join to the ring with a slst. Round 1: work 3 ch to replace the first dc (UK tr), then work 15 dc (UK tr) into the ring. Finish the round with 1 slst into the third replacement ch. Work rounds 2–6 to pattern 3.

Change colours and arrangements
Work the rows and rounds in the colours of your choice. To change a colour, join the new colour with 1 slst.

Gauge in basic pattern
22 stitches x 12 rows = 4 x 4in (10 x 10cm) ▶

HOW TO DO IT

For the back, work 79 ch + 3 turning ch, then work 48 rows to the basic pattern.

For the front, make a total of 16 squares. From square no. 2, join the squares together by working sc (UK dc) as indicated by an arrow on the previous square. Layout: 4 x 4 squares. Place the front and back together with the wrong sides facing, and crochet or sew along the side seams and the bottom. Work 4 rounds of the basic pattern along the top edge.

In round 5, work the openings for the handles as follows. Push the fabric bag inside the crocheted bag. Work 5 ch over 5 stitches of the previous round 4 times. Move the handles of the fabric bag to the front, work the chain arch behind the strap, and continue following the basic pattern. Work 2 more rounds in the basic pattern, including as appropriate over the 5 ch.

Finishing off: Hand sew the top edge to the inside of the fabric bag.

Crochet pattern 1   Crochet pattern 2

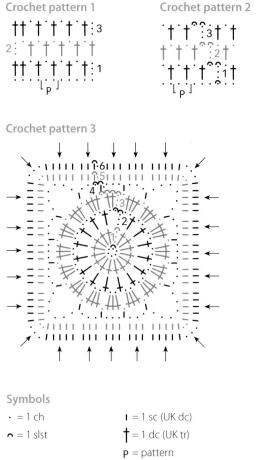

Crochet pattern 3

Symbols

• = 1 ch	I = 1 sc (UK dc)
∩ = 1 slst	† = 1 dc (UK tr)
	P = pattern

34

COLOURFUL STRIPED BAG

Size: approximately 11 x 9in (28 x 23cm) · Level of difficulty ●

Materials:
- Cotton yarn (100% cotton, length 76½yd/1¾oz, 70m/50g): 7oz (200g) in pink-orange-blue-light green
- G/6 (4mm, UK 8) crochet hook
- 1 button in a matching colour
- Sewing needle
- Sewing thread in a matching colour
- A little stiff card

Basic pattern

Work rows of sc (*UK dc*), with 1 ch at the beginning of each row to replace the first sc (*UK dc*).

Gauge

20 sc (*UK dc*) x 23 rows = 4 x 4in (10 x 10cm)

HOW TO DO IT

For the main part of the bag, work 120 ch + 1 turning ch. Work 9in (23cm) in the basic pattern, then finish. For the strap, work 224 ch + 1 turning ch. Rows 1–4: Work in the basic pattern, then finish.

Smooth the crocheted rectangle and fold the narrow bottom edge forward by 10¼in (26cm). Pin the strap 1¼in (3cm) down on the inside of both sides of the bag. Crochet the sides together with sc (*UK dc*), making sure you include the strap as well.

For the flap fold the top narrow side forward by 3¼in (7cm).

To make the button loop, attach the yarn to the flap ½in (1.5cm) from the front middle. Work 8 ch over the middle 1¼in (3cm), attach the chain arch with 1 slst, and then work 12 sc (*UK dc*) over the chain arch.

Make two tassels 3½in (9cm) long out of the crochet yarn. Cut a piece of card measuring 4¼ x 4¼in (11 x 11cm) and wind the yarn around it until it is of the desired thickness. Then wrap a double thread around one edge of the card and tie in a knot. Cut open the loops on the other side. Tie the bundle of threads ¾in (2cm) below the knot, wrap around several times and secure. Trim all the threads to the same length.

Finishing off: Sew the button onto the front to line up with the button loop. Sew the tassels to the bottom corners of the bag as seen in the photo.

Tip: With a few clever changes in materials, this casual model can be made into a glamorous party version for a smart evening out. Try making the bag out of black glitter yarn or another decorative yarn, attach a metal button and use a long metal chain (obtainable from DIY outlets) for the strap.

STRIPY LAUNDRY BAG

Size: 25½ x 23½in (65 x 60cm) · Level of difficulty ●

Materials:
- Cotton yarn (100% cotton, length 147yd/1¾oz, 135m/50g): 16oz (450g) in grass green, 10½oz (300g) in white, 5oz (150g) each in light blue, fuchsia and yellow
- J/10 (6mm, UK 4) crochet hook

Basic pattern
Work dc (*UK tr*) in rounds, starting each round with 3 ch to replace the first dc (*UK tr*), and ending with 1 slst into the third ch at the beginning of the round. To double 1 stitch, work 2 dc (*UK tr*) into the same stitch.

Stripy pattern
Turn after each round and start the next round with 3 or 1 ch to replace the first dc (*UK tr*) or sc (*UK dc*). Finish each round with 1 slst into the top of the ch at the beginning of the round. *3 rounds dc (*UK tr*) in grass green, 2 rounds sc (*UK dc*) in white, 3 rounds dc (*UK tr*) in light blue, 2 rounds sc (*UK dc*) in white, 3 rounds dc (*UK tr*) in yellow, 2 rounds sc (*UK dc*) in white, 3 rounds dc (*UK tr*) in fuchsia, 2 rounds sc (*UK dc*) in white, repeat once from *, finishing with 3 rounds of dc (*UK tr*) in grass green, 3 rounds sc (*UK dc*) in white, and one round of sc (*UK dc*) each in light blue, yellow, fuchsia, and grass green.

Gauge in basic pattern, three strands of yarn
11½ dc (*UK tr*) x 5 ½ rows = 4 x 4in (10 x 10cm)
Gauge in striped pattern, three strands of yarn
11½ stitches x 8 rows = 4 x 4in (10 x 10cm)

Note: Always use three strands of yarn.

HOW TO DO IT
For the **base** in grass green, work 6 ch and join in a ring with a slst. Work in the basic pattern as follows: **Round 1:** Work 15 dc (*UK tr*) in the ring. **Round 2:** Double every stitch = 30 dc (*UK tr*). **Round 3:** Double every second stitch = 45 dc (*UK tr*). **Round 4:** Double every third stitch = 60 dc (*UK tr*). **Round 5:** Double every fourth stitch = 75 dc (*UK tr*). **Round 6:** Double every fifth stitch = 90 dc (*UK tr*). **Round 7:** Double every sixth stitch = 105 dc (*UK tr*). **Round 8:** Double every seventh stitch = 120 dc (*UK tr*). **Round 9:** Double every eighth stitch = 135 dc (*UK tr*). **Round 10:** Continue without increasing. **Round 11:** Double every ninth stitch = 150 dc (*UK tr*). **Rounds 12–13:** Continue without increasing.
For the **body**, crochet the stripy pattern without increasing. In round 1, for the edge work the dc (*UK tr*) around the dc (*UK tr*) in the previous round rather than into the stitch (relief). After round 44 (approximately 21¾in/ 55cm) from the base work 28 dc (*UK tr*) for the handles, miss 19 dc (*UK tr*) with ch stitches, work 56 dc (*UK tr*), then work 19 ch over the next 19 dc (*UK tr*), and work the remaining 28 dc (*UK tr*). In the next round, work sc (*UK dc*) into the ch stitches. Finish after row 50 (approximately 23½in/60cm) from the base.

HANDBAG WITH DECORATIVE FLOWERS

Size: approximately 13 x 8¾in (33 x 22cm) · Level of difficulty ● ●

Materials:
- Synthetic blend (94% acrylic, 6% polyester, length 73yd/1¾oz, 67m/50g): 5oz (150g) in pastel orange marl
- Cotton yarn (100% cotton, length 76½yd (70m)/1¾oz (50g)): 1¾oz (50g) in red
- E/4 (3.5mm, UK 9) and G/6 (4mm, UK 8) crochet hooks
- 1 pair of bag handles and 4 matching D rings

Basic pattern

Work sc (*UK dc*) in rounds, but only into the back loop of the stitch. Start each round with 1 ch to replace the first sc (*UK dc*), and join to the starting ch with 1 slst to close.

Filet pattern

Work in rows as shown in pattern 1. Start each row with 3 ch to replace the first dc (*UK tr*). Start with the stitches before the pattern, work the pattern twice, and finish with the stitches after the pattern. Work rows 1–16.

HOW TO DO IT

For the two bag pieces, use the G/6 (4mm, UK8) hook and pastel orange marl to work 70 ch + 5 turning/replacement ch (grid 1), and work 16 rows in the filet pattern. Place the bag pieces together with the wrong sides facing and sew up the sides and base. Crochet the top bag trim in red to the bag using the E/4 (3.5mm, UK 9) hook. Cast 1 ch on along 1 side seam, then work 1 round of sc (*UK dc*), working 2 sc (*UK dc*) per grid, and close the round with 1 slst. Then work 7 more rounds in the basic pattern. Crochet 7 flowers in red to the bag pieces with the E/4 (3.5mm, UK9) hook.

Finishing off: Sew the bag handles and hangers to the red bag trim. ▶

Flowers

Work pattern 2 around an empty grid of the filet pattern, arranging the flowers as shown in pattern 1. Work the dc (*UK tr*) for a flower between the stitches or around the dc (*UK tr*) in the neighbouring grid.

Crochet pattern 1

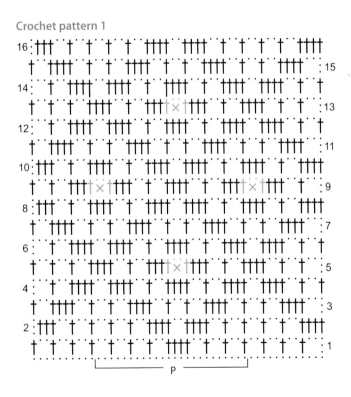

Crochet pattern 2

Symbols

· = 1 ch

∩ = 1 slst

I = 1 sc (UK dc)

† = 1 dc (UK tr)

P = pattern

X = position of the crocheted flower

ROUND BAG

Size: approximately 13½ x 13in (34 x 33cm) · Level of difficulty ● ●

Materials:

- Cotton yarn (100% cotton, length approximately 87yd/1¾oz, 80m/50g): 1¾oz (50g) each in turquoise, green, bright pink, orange and blue
- Plastic bag handles in orange, 5¾ x 4¼in (14.5 x 11cm)
- 7 (4.5mm, UK 7) or H/8 (5mm, UK 6) crochet hook
- Thick sewing needle

Basic pattern

Work in rows to the pattern. Start each row with 3 additional ch. Work the dc (*UK tr*) between the stitches rather than into them. The pattern is only drawn for rows 1–4.

Work rows 5–14 in the same way for the number of stitches in the instructions. Work the increases evenly over the rounded section. For each increase, work 2 dc (*UK tr*) into 1 stitch. Change the colour after each straight row.

Gauge in basic pattern

15 dc (*UK tr*) x 10 rows = 4 x 4in (10 x 10cm) ▶

HOW TO DO IT

For the front, work 10 ch in turquoise. Row 1 (right side):
Follow the basic pattern and diagram: 3 ch, 9 dc (*UK tr*), work
6 dc (*UK tr*) into the tenth ch, then work 9 dc (*UK tr*) down the
other side of the line of ch = 25 stitches.

Row 2 (wrong side): 3 ch, 9 dc (*UK tr*), double 5 dc (*UK tr*), 10
dc (*UK tr*) = 30 stitches. Row 3: Work 3 ch in orange, 10 dc (*UK
tr*), double 8 dc (*UK tr*), 11 dc (*UK tr*) = 38 stitches. Row 4: Work
in orange without increasing. Row 5: Work 3 ch in pink, 15 dc
(*UK tr*), double 6 dc (*UK tr*), 16 dc (*UK tr*) = 44 stitches. Row 6:
3 ch, 18 dc (*UK tr*), double 6 dc (*UK tr*), 19 dc (*UK tr*) = 50
stitches. Row 7: Work in green without increasing. Row 8: 3
ch, 20 dc (*UK tr*), double 9 dc (*UK tr*), 21 dc (*UK tr*) = 60 stitches.
Rows 9–10: Work in turquoise without increasing. Row 11:
Work in orange without increasing. Row 12: 3 ch, 19 dc (*UK
tr*), double 20 dc (*UK tr*), 20 dc (*UK tr*) = 80 stitches. Row 13:
Work in blue without increasing. Row 14: 3 ch, 38 dc (*UK tr*),
double 2 dc (*UK tr*), 39 dc (*UK tr*) = 82 stitches. Work the back
in the same way.

Place the front and back together with the wrong sides
facing. Row 15: Work in bright pink without increasing,
pushing the hook under the stitch segments of both parts
to join them together = 82 stitches.

Make the top edge of the front and back separately. Do this
with sc (*UK dc*) in right and wrong side rows in the following
colours: Rows 1–2: In blue. Rows 3–4: In bright pink. Rows
5–6: In orange. Rows 7–8: In turquoise. Rows 9–10: In green.
Rows 11–12: In blue. Finally, work 1 row of sc (*UK dc*) in
turquoise along the edge stitches, then finish.

Finishing off: Sew the handles to the front and back as
shown in the photo.

Crochet pattern

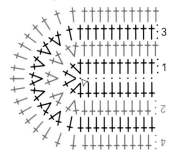

Symbols

$\triangle$ = start here

· = 1 ch

† = 1 dc (*UK tr*)

Ⅴ = 2 dc (*UK tr*) in same stitch

GREEN SHOPPER BAG

Size: approximately 15¾ x 9¾in (40 x 25cm) · Level of difficulty ●

Materials:

- Cotton yarn (100% cotton, length approximately 98yd/1¾oz, 90m/50g): 5oz (150g) in grey, 3½oz (100g) in lime, 3½oz (100g) in anthracite, 3½oz (100g) in grass green, 3½oz (100g) in black, 1¾oz (50g) in light green
- G/6 (4mm, UK 8) crochet hook

Basic pattern

Sc (*UK dc*) in rounds (spiral transition).

Colour sequence

Two rounds each in *grey, lime, anthracite, grass green, black, light green, repeating from * and pulling the yarn from the colour changes up (change colours at the sides).

Gauge

16 sc (*UK dc*) x 20 rows = 4 x 4in (10 x 10cm)

HOW TO DO IT

For the base, work 49 ch in grey, then work 7in (18cm) in rows, working 1 ch for the transition to the next round.

For the sides, work 142 stitches in grey around the base, then continue working in rounds to the basic pattern in stripes until the work measures 9¾in (25cm). Divide the top edge as follows, making sure that the transition is at the side. Omit the middle 37 stitches on each wide side, and work across the remaining 34 stitches between them. In the next round, instead of the uncrocheted stitches, work 116 ch for the strap. Work another 2in (5cm) in the basic pattern, then finish.

MOTTLED GREEN BASKET BAG

Size: approximately 15 x 15in (38 x 38cm) • Level of difficulty ● ●

Materials:
- Cotton yarn (100% cotton, length 136yd/1¾oz, 125m/50g): 5oz (150g) each in mottled green, off-white and khaki
- D/3 (3mm, UK 11) Tunisian crochet hook

Basic pattern
Work sc (UK dc) in continuous rounds without a beginning or end. Mark the round transitions with a piece of thread. For each increase, work 2 sc (UK dc) into 1 stitch. When changing colours, finish the last stitch in one colour in the new colour.

Tunisian crochet pattern
The pattern consists of a right side row and a wrong side row. You always work on the front side; do not turn the work at the end of a row. Row 1 (right side): 1 ch, insert hook in each ch and pull through 1 loop, leaving all the loops on the hook. Do not turn. Row 2 (wrong side): 1 ch, then gradually work through all the loops: yarn around hook, and draw through 2 loops. Continue in this fashion until you have 1 loop left on the hook.
Row 3 (right side): Insert hook under the horizontal thread of each stitch in the previous row and pull through 1 loop. Row 4 (wrong side): Work as row 2.
Work rows 1–4 once, then keep repeating rows 3 and 4.

Gauge in basic pattern, two strands of yarn
18 sc (UK dc) x 18 rows = 4 x 4in (10 x 10cm)

Note: Work with two strands of yarn.

HOW TO DO IT
For the bag base, work 2 ch in khaki, then work 7 sc (UK dc) into the first ch (round 1), then continue working to the basic pattern, alternating between 1 round in off-white and 1 round in khaki. Round 2: Double every stitch = 14 stitches.
Round 3: Double every second stitch = 21 sc (UK dc). Rounds 4–21: In every round, increase 7 stitches in the same places = 147 sc (UK dc). Rounds 22–36: Continue working without increasing. In round 22, insert hook in back of stitch only. Rounds 37–54: Working in mottled green, *1 dc (UK tr), 1 ch, miss 1 stitch, repeat from *, moving the pattern along by 1 stitch in every round. Round 55: Sc (UK dc) in off-white. Round 56: Sc (UK dc) in khaki.
For the straps make 6 ch, then work 9¾in (25cm) in Tunisian crochet. Fold the strip in half lengthways and slst together. Make 1 strap in off-white and 1 in khaki.
Finishing off: Sew the straps to the top of the bag about 5½in (14cm) apart.

HANDBAG WITH DOUBLE STRAP

Size: approximately 13 x 9½in (33 x 24cm) · Level of difficulty ● ●

Materials:
- Cotton blend – 55% cotton, 45% polyacrylic, length 98yd (90m)/1¾oz (50g): 3½oz (100g) each in black and white
- M/13 (9mm, UK 000) crochet hook
- Sewing needle
- Black sewing thread

Basic pattern 1
Work rows of sc (*UK dc*), with 1 ch at the beginning of each row to replace the first sc (*UK dc*). If working in rounds, end the round with 1 slst into the replacement ch.

Basic pattern 2
Work dc (*UK tr*) in rounds, starting each row with 3 ch to replace the first dc (*UK tr*), and ending the round with 1 slst into the third replacement ch.

Note: Work with two strands of yarn.

HOW TO DO IT
For the front and back work 14 ch + 1 turning ch in black, then crochet 7 rows in basic pattern 1. Miss or decrease 1 stitch on both sides of every second row. Continue working in rounds to basic pattern 1. Round 1: In black, and working 1 hdc (*UK htr*), 1 dc (*UK tr*) and 1 hdc (*UK htr*) into the top corner stitches. Rounds 2–5: In white, and working the bottom corner stitches as before, work 3 sc (*UK dc*) into the top corners, in round 2 between the 2 corner stitches, in rounds 3–5 in the right corner before the middle corner stitch, in the left corner after the corner stitch. Rounds 6–7: Work as rounds 3–5, but in black.

Round 8: Working in black and to basic pattern 2, work 3 dc (*UK tr*) in the top corners, and 1 dc (*UK tr*), one trc (*UK dtr*) and 1 more dc (*UK tr*) into the bottom corners.
For the side, work 8 ch + 1 turning ch in white. Crochet 29¼in (74cm) of sc (*UK dc*) in rows to basic pattern 1, then crochet 1 round of sc (*UK dc*) in black around the side. Place between the front and back, and slst together.
For the straps, work 2 lines of ch stitches about 43¼in (110cm) long in black. Sew the ends of the straps to the side edges of the front and back, starting and finishing at the bottom corner.

Tip: If you like more of a contrast, you could make one strap in white and the other in black – or use a completely different colour for the straps. The lovely shape of this bag also looks just as striking in other colour combinations, such as dark red with beige or chocolate with turquoise.

STRIPED BAG

Size: approximately 13½ x 13¾in (34 x 35cm) • Level of difficulty ●

Materials:
- Cotton blend (60% cotton, 40% acrylic, length approximately 76½yd/1¾oz , 70m/50g): 1¾oz (50g) each in light blue, navy, purple and aquamarine
- H/8 (5mm, UK 6) crochet hook
- Thick sewing needle

Basic pattern

Work dc (*UK tr*) in rows, starting each row with 3 ch to replace the first dc (*UK tr*). Work only into the back loop of the stitch (on the front), and the front loop of the stitch (on the back).

Gauge

13 dc (*UK tr*) x 7 rows = 4 x 4in (10 x 10cm)

HOW TO DO IT

For the front, work 46 ch in light turquoise, then continue in the basic pattern in the following colours. Rows 1–6: In light blue. Rows 7–12: In navy. Rows 13–18: In purple. Row 19: Continue working in aquamarine. For the handle slit work 12 dc (*UK tr*), 22 ch, 12 dc (*UK tr*). Rows 20–24: Work in the basic pattern. Make the back in the same way. Finishing off: Place the front and back together with the right sides facing, and slst together. Turn the bag right side out.

BOOK BAG

Size: approximately 13¾ x 10¾in (35 x 27cm) · Level of difficulty ● ●

Materials:
- Cotton blend (60% cotton, 40% acrylic, length approximately 76½yd/1¾oz, 70m/50g): 10½oz (300g) in grey
- Cotton yarn (100% cotton, length approximately 180yd/1¾oz, 165m/50g): scraps in bright pink
- 78¾in (200cm) webbing in bright pink, 2in (5cm) wide
- H/8 (5mm, UK 6) crochet hook

Basic pattern
Work dc (*UK tr*) in rows, starting each row with 3 ch to replace the first dc (*UK tr*).

Gauge
13 dc (*UK tr*) x 7 rows = 4 x 4in (10 x 10cm)

HOW TO DO IT
For the front, work 49 ch in grey, then 20 rows in the basic pattern. For the back, work 49 ch in grey, then 20 rows in the basic pattern.

Row 21 (start of the flap): Cast off the first 3 dc (*UK tr*), then work 43 dc (*UK tr*), and omit the last 3 stitches. Rows 22–30: Work in the basic pattern. Row 31: Work 1 row of sc (*UK dc*) in bright pink, then finish.

For the base, 7 ch in grey, then work 21 rows in the basic pattern.

Finishing off: Place the back and front together with the wrong sides facing. Slst the sides together (the seams will be on the outside). Sew the base into place along the two long sides, leaving the short sides open. Insert one end of the webbing into each narrow edge, and secure in the middle over the side seam of the bag. Use zigzag stitch and grey thread to machine sew the webbing to the bag.

COLOURFUL GRANNY SQUARE BAG

Size: 13½ x 13½ x 4¼in (34 x 34 x 11cm) • Level of difficulty ● ● ●

Materials:

- Cotton blend (50% cotton, 50% acrylic microfibre, length approximately 134½yd/1¾oz, 123m/50g): 3½oz (100g) each in pale pink, orange, pine, apple green, lilac and violet, 1¾oz (50g) each in cream, reseda green, flame red, cherry, grass green and gold
- 7 (4.5mm, UK 7) and H/8 (5mm, UK 6) crochet hooks
- Sequin or rhinestone ribbons (for the straps), alternatively 1 pair of bag handles
- Small sequins and rocailles
- Darning or embroidery needle
- Sewing needle, thread in a matching colour

Basic pattern

Work rows of dc (*UK tr*), starting each round with 3 ch to replace the first dc (*UK tr*).

Note: Work with two strands of yarn.

HOW TO DO IT

For the **body for the bag**, make 24 squares as shown in the diagram with the H/8 (5mm, UK6) hook. For the squares, work rounds 1 and 2 in one colour, round 3 in another colour, and round 4 in a third colour as shown, or else to suit your own taste. Then work 1 round of sc (*UK dc*) around each square in pink, orange or apple green, working 1 sc (*UK dc*) into each stitch, and 3 sc (*UK dc*) into each corner stitch. Finish the round with 1 slst.

For the **base**, work 16 ch in pine with the 4.5mm (US7, UK7) hook and follow the basic pattern. Finish after 24 rows. Sew sequins and rocailles onto the squares. Insert the needle through one sequin and one rocaille, then around the rocaille and back to the sequin. ▶

Crochet pattern

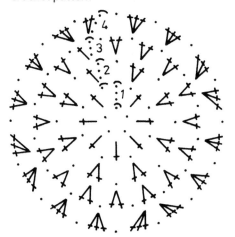

Finishing off: Arrange the 24 squares in 3 rows of 8 in any way you like. Using a double thread of the same colour as the border colour of the square, sew the squares together using whip stitch, but only going through the back section of the border stitches. Sew the short sides of the webbing together and join in a ring. Put the base into place. Using the H/8 (5mm, UK6) hook, crochet 2 rounds of sc (*UK dc*) in pine around the top of the bag. Sew the straps to the middle of the inner squares.

Tip: For a more rustic effect, sew wooden beads onto the bag and use leather straps.

Symbols

• = 1 ch

∩ = 1 slst

† = 1 dc (*UK tr*)

If the symbols are joined at the bottom, this means the stitches are worked into the same stitch of the previous round.

PATTERNED BAG WITH GOLD CHAIN

Size: approximately 11¾ x 7 x 4¾in (30 x 18 x 12cm) • Level of difficulty ● ● ●

Materials:
- Cotton blend (70% cotton, 30% polyamide, length 98yd/1¾oz, 90m/50g): 8¾oz (250g) in light green and 5oz (150g) in teal
- H/8 (5mm, UK 6) crochet hook
- 2 sew-on magnetic catches in silver, ¾in (18mm) diameter
- 1 chain with end hooks in gold, 27½in (70cm) long
- Firm cardboard for the base, approximately 4 x 11¾in (10 x 30cm)
- Blunt embroidery needle

Basic pattern

Work rows of sc (*UK dc*), turning at the end of each row with 1 additional ch.

Gauge in basic pattern

12 sc (*UK dc*) x 13 rows/rounds= 4 x 4in (10 x 10cm)
1 crocheted square = 4 x 4in (10 x 10cm)

Note: Work with two strands of yarn.

Crocheted square

Work in rounds to the diagram, working round 1 in light green into a yarn loop. Round 1 is shown in full. Start each round with 1 ch to replace the first sc (*UK dc*) and the stitches before the pattern repeat. Work the pattern three times, then finish with the stitches before the round change, and 1 slst in the replacement ch.
When changing colours, finish the slst in the new colour. Work rounds 1–6 once, with round 1 in light green, rounds 2 and 3 in teal, rounds 4 and 5 in light green, and round 6 in teal. Tighten the yarn loop in the middle.

Joining the motifs

Place the motifs you wish to join close together, right sides facing down. Sew the motifs together in teal along the outer edges, inserting the needle through only the top part of the sc (*UK dc*) and using whip stitch. The front parts of the sc (*UK dc*) remain loose on the front of the work.

HOW TO DO IT

For the back and flap, crochet 12 squares and join them together in a rectangle of 3 x 4 squares. Leave a ½in (1cm) opening between the back and the flap on both sides so you can pull the chain through (see • in the diagram on page 60). To make the front, crochet 6 squares and join in a rectangle of 3 x 2 squares.

For the base, work 36 ch + 1 turning ch in light green, and crochet in accordance with the basic pattern. Finish after row 14 from the beginning (approximately 4¼in/11cm).

For the sides (make 2), crochet 13 ch + 1 turning ch in light green, and crochet in accordance with the basic pattern. Finish after row 26 from the beginning (approximately 7¾in/20cm). ▶

For the handle, make 8 ch in light green and join in a ring with 1 slst. Work in rounds to the basic pattern, starting each round with 1 replacement ch for the first sc (UK dc), and finishing with 1 slst into the replacement ch. Finish after row 19 (approximately 5¾in/14.5cm) from the beginning.

For the bag eyelet (make 2), crochet 4 ch in teal and join in a ring with 1 slst. Work 17 sc (UK dc) into the ring, with 1 ch to replace the first sc (UK dc) and finishing with 1 slst into the first ch.

Finishing off: Working on the outside, slst the bottom edges of the front and back to the opposite long sides of the base in teal, working the slst around the stitch loops of the last round of the crochet squares, and around the stitch loops of the basic pattern at the same time if possible, so that the 'seam' is visible on the outside of the bag.

Crochet the short edges of the side pieces to the short pieces of the base. Work slst down the sides of the front and back in teal, as described earlier.

Sew the eyelets 1in (2.5cm) on either side in the middle of the outside of the bag. Draw the chain through the eyelets and attach the hooks to the bag to secure.

Sew the tops of the magnetic button to the corners of the inside of the bag flap, ½in (1cm) from the edges. Sew the bottoms to the corresponding areas on the front of the bag. Place the cardboard in the bottom of the bag.

Crochet pattern 1

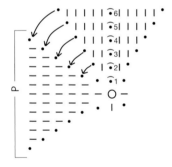

Crochet pattern 2

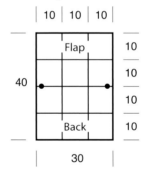

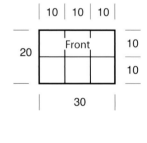

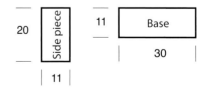

Symbols

O = yarn in a loop

• = 1 ch

⌒ = 1 slst

I = 1 sc (UK dc)

P = pattern

SHOULDER BAG WITH SQUARE BASE

Size: approximately 8¼ x 8¼ x 9in (21 x 21 x 23cm) • Level of difficulty ● ●

Materials:

- Cotton blend (97% cotton, 3% polyester, length 136¾yd/1¾oz, 125m/50g): 7oz (200g) in bright pink
- 1 pair leather bag handles, 19¾in (50cm) long
- 2 pieces bright pink fleece approximately 9 x 9in (23 x 23cm)
- Firm cardboard (for the base), 8¼ x 8¼in (21 x 21cm)
- 7 (4.5mm, UK 7) and H/8 (5mm, UK 6) crochet hook
- Thick sewing or strong needle
- Sewing thread in a matching colour
- Leather adhesive

Basic pattern

Work in rows to the pattern. Start uneven rows with 1 ch to replace the first sc (*UK dc*). Start even rows with 3 ch to replace the first dc (*UK tr*). Start with the stitches before the pattern, and keep repeating the pattern to the end of the row. Repeat rows 1 to 9.

Crochet pattern

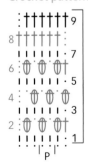

Symbols

- · = 1 ch
- I = 1 sc (*UK dc*)
- † = 1 dc (*UK tr*)
- ⬮ = dec 3 dc (*UK tr*) tog in the same stitch
- P = pattern

Gauge

15 dc (*UK tr*) x 10 rows = 4 x 4in (10 x 10cm)

HOW TO DO IT

To make a side piece (make 2), crochet 75 ch and work 27 rows (3 repeats) in the basic pattern, then finish.

For the base, work 32 ch + 3 turning ch and work 21 rows of dc (*UK tr*).

Finishing off: Place the side pieces together with the right sides facing. Slip stitch together. Sew the base into the bottom edge with the right sides facing. Turn the bag right side out. Sew 1 row of dc (*UK tr*) and 1 row of sc (*UK dc*) around the top of the bag, then finish.

Secure the bag handles by brushing leather adhesive over the back of the leather flap and pushing them firmly into place (see photo). The ends of the leather handles should be approximately 9½in (24cm) apart from each other. Leave the adhesive to dry, then secure the ends with a strong needle and thick thread.

For the base, place the pieces of fleece together with the right sides facing, then machine sew along three sides with a seam allowance of ½in (1cm). Turn right side out and iron. Push the card into the sleeve. Fold the seam allowances to the inside and sew up the turning opening by hand. Put the base in the bag.

Publication details

First published in Great Britain in 2015 by
Search Press Limited
Wellwood, North Farm Road,
Tunbridge Wells, Kent TN2 3DR

Original edition © 2014
World rights reserved by Christophorus Verlag GmbH,
Freiburg/Germany
Original German title: *Bunte Taschen Häkeln!*

English translation by Burravoe Translation Services

Design and projects: Coats Design (pages 36–37, 40–42), Drops
Design (pages 26–27), Stefanie Hanisch (pages 48–49), Junghans
Wollversand (pages 10–11, 12–15, 38–39), Lang Yarns (pages 56–58),
Heidi Opitz (pages 30–32), OZ-Archiv (pages 16–17, 50–51), Elke Reith
(pages 43–45, 52–55, 62–63), Sabine Ruf (pages 59–61), Sabine
Schidelko (pages 8–9, 20–25, 33–35), Schoeller + Stahl (pages 46–47),
Dagmar Scholz (pages 28–29), Carolin Schwarberg (pages 18–19)
Photography: : Coats Design (page 41), Drops Design (page 27), Uli
Glasemann (pages 11, 39), Junghans Wolle (page 13), Lang Yarns
(page 57), Rainer Muranyi (pages 9, 21–25, 33–35, 43–45, 53–55, 63),
Petra Obermüller (pages 17, 31), Christine Rosinski (pages 19, 29),
Peter Münnich (page 61), Uzwei Fotodesign (pages 37, 47),
Fotostudio Wehinger (page 49), OZ-Archiv (page 51)
Styling: Shumita Choudhuri (pages 9, 21–25, 33–35, 43–45, 53–55,
63), Coats Design (page 41), Drops Design (page 27), Christiane
Käsmayr (pages 36–37), Lang Yarns (page 57), Christine Oesterle
(pages 17, 31), Elke Reith (pages 11, 39), Claudia Rittich (pages 19,
29), Karin Schlag (pages 13, 47, 49), OZ-Archiv (page 51)
Crochet patterns: Carsten Bachmann (pages 44, 62), Sabine
Schidelko (pages 22, 28, 32, 42, 43, 60)

ISBN 978-1-78221-222-5

Printed in China

Suppliers

If you have difficulty in obtaining any of the materials and
equipment mentioned in this book, then please visit the Search
Press website for details of suppliers: www.searchpress.com.